□RICHER Press

An Imprint of Richer Life, LLC

RICHER Press is a full service, specialty Trade publisher whose sole goal is to shape thoughts and change lives for the better. All of the books, eBooks and digital media we publish, distribute and market embrace our commitment to help maximize opportunities for personal growth and professional achievement.

To learn more visit

www.richerlifellc.com

Copyright © 2014 by Tiny Stallings-Clark

Published by RICHER Press
An Imprint of Richer Life, LLC

4600 E. Washington Street, Suite 300, Phoenix, Arizona 85034
www.richerlifellc.com

Cover Design: Richer Media USA • Photographs: Big Stock Photo

No part of this publication may be reproduced, stored in a retrieval system, or transmitted in any form or by any means, electronic, mechanical, photocopying, recording, scanning, or otherwise, except as permitted under Section 107 or 108 of the 1976 United States Copyright Act, without prior written permission of the publisher.

Library of Congress Cataloging-in-Publications Data

I Choose To Live
Tiny Stallings-Clark. -- 1st edition
p.   cm.

1. Poetry   2. Self Help   3. Inspiration
ISBN 978-0-9855699-1-4 (pbk : alk. Paper)

2013944880—Paperback Version

ISBN 13: 978-0-9899001-9-5

ISBN 10: 0-9899001-9-5

Text set is Trebuchet MS

PRINTED IN THE UNITED STATES OF AMERICA

First Edition
February 2014

DEDICATION

This book is dedicated to my Mother, who is a cancer survivor and whose walk in faith exemplifies the hymn "On This Solid Rock I Stand", my three children who continued to believe in me, my best friend Toni who has always had faith in me and who went beyond the cause to encourage me to continue to focus on the end results.

I would also like to make a special dedication to my Dad whose travels on this road of life ended in July 1990. To my Aunt Marie Brown who won her battle with cancer in July 1988. Before ending her travel on this road of life she left these words of advice, "Always take care of *self* first and love each moment of life to its fullest. When *self* is taken care of, then...you can give."

CONTENTS

PREFACE   7

PART ONE - THINGS
When You Think Life's Over...Well It's Not   11
At The Lowest Point In Life   13
Life's Circumstances   15
Deep Scars   17
Was It Worth It   19

PART TWO - TIMES OF HURT AND CONFUSION
Reaching Out   23
Pillar of Strength   25
Stepping Stone   27
You Are   29
Let God   31
You Did   33
My Focal Point   35
I Am Everything   37

PART THREE - STEPS TO RECOVERY
Me   41
I Dared   43
My Feet March To A Different Beat   45
Our Dreams And Our Goals   47

CONTENTS

PART FOUR - SETBACKS AND CHALLENGES

Escape	51
Recycling Life	53
Quiet My Mind So That I May Hear	55
It's Gonna Be Okay	57

PART FIVE - NEGATIVITY

Closing The Door To Negativity	61
Negativity	63

PART SIX - THE PROCESS TO RECOVERY

Achieving Balance	67
Achieving Well Being	69
Loving Yourself First	71
One Day At A Time	73
Ground Yourself in God's Word	75
Build a Relationship With God	77

PART SEVEN - CHOOSING TO LIVE

This Road I Travel	81
I Choose To Live	83

About The Author	85

PREFACE

This book is being written for all women going through circumstances in life, which are causing them to feel alone and hopeless.

It is intended to give hope to the hopeless and a new outlook on life to those who still struggle with the past. If you allow yourself to look beyond the existing problems and focus on God's written word — *"Let us lay aside every weight, and the sin which doth so easily beset us, and let us run with patience the race that our faith: who for the joy that set before him endured the cross, despising the shame, and is set down at the right hand of the throne of God"* (Hebrew 12: 1-2) — then you will discover that there exists a "life force" deep within to guide you through the difficult times. You will also come to understand this force and realize that it was originated from a power source that is bigger and greater than any force found on this earth. It is a gift that is allowed to be passed through each and every one of us.

"I Choose to Live" contains food for thought in the form of personal poems of inspirations, messages encountered through scripture, personal experiences as well as lessons taught me by fellow travelers on this road of life. As a fellow traveler, I want to pass on to you...my weary travelers...hope and peace. I also want to ensure you that your travel will not have been in vain. *You will* and *you can* survive and *you won't* be alone!

Now soar beyond what may seem to be an impossible dream. *God Bless.* And I'll meet you at the top.

PART ONE

THINGS

WHEN THINGS HAPPEN AND LIFE DEALS YOU A BAD HAND, STOPS YOU IN YOUR TRACKS, MAKES YOU FEEL HOPELESS AND HELPLESS...THERE IS STILL HOPE.

YOU CAN GO ON. YOU WILL SURVIVE.

WHEN YOU THINK LIFE'S OVER... WELL IT'S NOT

"I can do all things through Christ which strengthens me."
(Philippians 4:13)

When you think life's over and you think you can't go any further, *It's not* and *you will*. Even when you are at your lowest, you still have more to give. Just as you find different ways to reuse materials when it's original purpose no longer exist, we can do the same thing with our lives. When God created us, it was with a purpose, and because of this I do not believe that once we have been dealt a few bad hands in life that we should simply give up on life and call it quits.

Look at life this way...like everything else in this world, there are many ups and downs --- there is a natural recycling process which leads to a rebound. Things will eventually get better. Keeping this in mind, we should not be surprised during our journey through life; we can expect a similar process in our own life. It's not going to be easy. But, if we can look at everything that happens in our life as a growing process and accept the many challenges we encounter as the stepping stones to recovery, with the help of God, we will survive...if we want it bad enough.

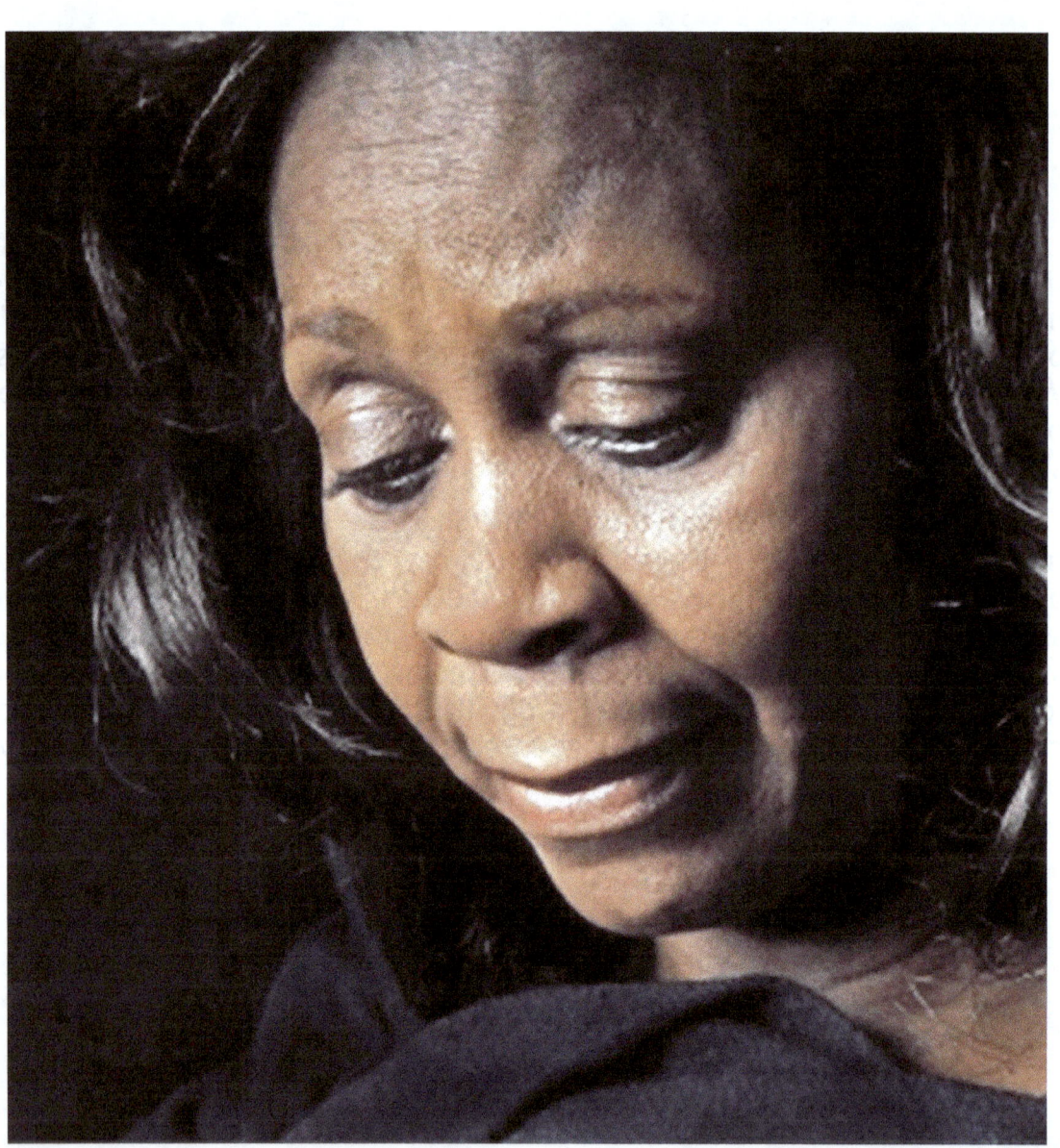

AT THE LOWEST POINT IN LIFE

At the lowest point in my life, when I could not control life's circumstances, life seemed to be one big stomachache. I was burnt out and I thought I was not going to get through this personal growth period. Then, one day I decided to *let go of it all and I began channeling the power within*. I physically and mentally released everything within. When I decided to do this, I began to experience the breath of life once again...just like an infant baby. I had to learn to crawl first before I could walk. Next, I began to take those first baby steps; a little off balance, and not perfect. Eventually, I started to walk again. Now, I was not afraid of taking that next step forward in life. I now knew that my steps were being guided by a pro and I was not taking life steps by myself. I had the best and the most powerful source there is to have...I had God!

Now, I am experiencing life differently and I see life through a new set of eyes. Life never look better...and it feels good! Remember that, life is never going to be what we expect it to be. But, I thank God that when life gets so bad and rotten in my mind, I have Him to lean on.

"We lose the fire, that burning desire to continue on."

LIFE'S CIRCUMSTANCES

Sometime life's circumstances will deal us a hand that causes us to fall short of our mission. We lose the fire, that burning desire to continue on. Because of this, we tend to become stagnant and end up standing still while the world continues on. We appear to wander in a daze going in slow motion. We no longer interact, we react. We find ourselves falling short of our dreams, feeling hopeless and full of self-doubt.

DEEP SCARS

How many scars do you hold...
old ones...
new ones...
anciently passed on ones.
Scars that are so bold that they will never be told.
Scars that cry out why
And are etched...way deep within the soul.
Scars that cannot be mended,
with a simple stitch of a needle...
A kind word never spoken or uttered,
a simple smile never shown for approval.
Only a nasty look,
which meant disapproval.
Scars torched and branded deep within the skin...
making it a sin...to love self...to forgive self...
even to look at self.
Scars that can only be mended with
...self-acceptance,
...self-approval,
...self-forgiveness,
...self-love,
...self.

"When all is said and done, was it worth it?"

WAS IT WORTH IT

When all is said and done, was it worth it?
When all is said and done was the lying...
The deceitfulness...the yelling
...the fighting...the screaming...the sadness...the madness
...the pain...the hurting...the crying
...the moaning...the suffering...the dying.
Was it worth it?
When all is said and done.

PART TWO
TIMES OF HURT AND CONFUSION

WHO YOU CAN DEPEND ON IN THIS TIME OF HURT AND CONFUSION

"I reached out my heart and your heart was now mine."

REACHING OUT

This day I awaken to find myself falling.
I reached out my hand and you grabbed it tight.
With all of your might you reached deep down inside
and found the strength to keep me on my feet.
I reached out my soul and you made it whole.
I reached out my heart and your heart was now mine.

I thought I had lost this upward climb, but...
God gave me you...a very small piece of himself
to see me through.

PILLAR OF STRENGTH

I'll be your pillar of strength when all else fails.

I'll be there to hear your cries of anguish when no one else is listening.

And when the pain becomes so great that you cannot bear it...I'll lift you up high and keep you there until there is pain no more.

I'll soothe and heal your wounds;

Then I will listen to all of your problems until they too are problems no more.

I'll be your pillar of strength throughout the wakening hours.

And as the night falls upon your face,

I'll be the Pillar you rest your head on throughout the sleeping night.

"For the path you travel was paved and designed for each step you choose to take."

STEPPING STONE

I'll be your stepping stone.
I'll be there with you each step of the way.
You might not sense my presence,
But the moment the breath of life was breathed into you;
The rough stones in preparation for your life journey were made smooth.

Remember what I promised you.
I will be there with you through the bad times as well as the good times.
Don't wait with doubt.
Step out on faith and let me lead the way.
Then you will see how simple life's steps can be.

For the path you travel was paved and designed for each step you choose to take.

Always have me in your thoughts,
And when you reach a cross-road along the way, even when you think you know the way…stop and always ask for guidance…

I'll be that stepping-stone either way you choose to go.

YOU ARE

You are the breath that I take,
...the air that I breathe.
You are the wind against my face,
...the water that I thirst.
You are the sleep that I yearn,
...the mere images of my dreams.
You are everything to me.

You are the words to my songs,
...and the lyrics that I sing.
You are the joy that I feel,
...my hope for tomorrow.
You are the laughter in my voice,
...the very beat of my heart.
You are everything to me.

Storms will arise,
tears may cloud my eyes;
But, the love of God will never die.

"Let the whole spirit of God be within you."

LET GOD

When you feel you can't live anymore...
Let God live within you,
Let God be your focal point,
Let God be your sight,
Let God be your messenger,
Let God be your receiver,
Let God be your giver,
Let God be your comforter,
Let the whole spirit of God be within you.

YOU DID

When no one else could soothe the pain,
feel the shame,
left by the chains,
inflicted by the not so sane;
Who often took our hearts and souls in vain,
almost causing us to go insane...
You did.

When no one else would take the time,
to hold the hands,
that were not so pretty;
Caused by the shattered hopes and dreams of tomorrow,
raked by the hurts and scars left from afar...
You did.

When no one else made a difference;
Because of not daring to dare.
When all it took was just a little caring...
Not being concerned with the circumstances,
that come with the act of baring which comes so naturally
with the gift of sharing...
You did.

My Focal Point

My focal point.
The center of my gravity,
the essence of my existence…
Holding me at bay.
The balancing force in my life,
that keeps my feet steady,
that keeps me from faltering,
when this force is not in play….
My journey through life starts to sway.

I AM YOUR EVERYTHING

I am Alpha ...the beginning. I am the key to your life....call out to me and I will hear your cries and your desires for peace and tranquility. I will enable you to endure all challenges.

Your hope will be the hope that I will supply and your desires will be the desires I have for you. Your heart will be full of joy and happiness and it will last a lifetime. The joy and peace that I have for you will be everlasting.

I will comfort you and give your mind rest. You will grow and learn to conquer defeat.

The pain that comes into your life will last only for a short time. I will guide you through the turmoil, the hurt and the pain. I will enable you to endure to the end.

I am the word and my word is the truth. I am just and I am righteous...I am that and that is that...that is yet to come.

I am your right hand...I am your left hand. I am your arms...I am your legs...I am your feet. I am your mouth...I am the air you breathe in.

I am your conscious....I am your mind. I am your all...I am your everything.
I am day...I am night...I am the sun...I am the moon...

My name is your name...my wealth is your wealth. My all is your all, so be fearful and anxious for nothing, but be hopeful and expectant of all that is to come.

Call out my name and I will hear your cries through all confusion and turmoil.

I am the omega....the End. You can lean on me when you are at your weakest and I will carry you through.

I am your everything.

PART THREE
STEPS TO RECOVERY

TAKING THE FIRST STEPS TO RECOVERY

"There are parts of me that are glad... and there are parts of me that are sad."

ME

There are parts of me that are real...
and there are parts of me I won't ever reveal.

There are parts of me I want to show...
and there are parts of me that I will not show.

There are parts of me that are glad...
and there are parts of me that are sad.

There are parts of me that want to shout...*let me out*,
and there are parts of me with lots of doubt.

There are parts of me that are just plain scared...
and there are parts of me that *just don't give a care!*
There are parts of me that can't say *no*,
and parts of me that say...let me go.

There are parts of me that give and take and give and take...
and eventually give way.

I DARED

You came into my life and
I dared to smile.

You came into my life and
I dared to laugh.

You came into my life and
I dared to be me...
I dared to trust once more.

I dared to believe the unbelievable,
...to fly high above the clouds,
...to reach for the unreachable,
...to dream the inconceivable
...to think the unthinkable,
I dared to be free!

MY FEET MARCH TO A DIFFERENT BEAT

My feet march to a different beat...
never ever succumbing to defeat;
And if my feet just happen to skip a beat...
I'll just shuffle my feet to adjust to the tempo.

The rhythm I march.... to is a steadfast beat.
A beat that cries out loud and strong;
..."Here's to victory."

A beat that challenges defeat head-on.

A beat that calls out with pride to those who have come before me .

For you see, my feet march to a different beat...
never ever succumbing to this...
"so-called defeat! "

OUR DREAMS AND OUR GOALS

We all have dreams and we all have goals that we set. Sometimes because of the a lack of direction, a lack of confidence, a lack of motivation, a lack of support, or that extra push and affirmation from someone else, things prevent us from taking that next step in achieving the "dream or goal" we dared think possible....We place everything that has to do with obtaining that dream on hold or we develop the mindset that "our dream is unattainable and that it will probably never happen anyway." As a result, that dream...that goal never comes to fruition.

At some point in our lives, I feel that deep down inside of our inner being and core, there lay a dream and this inkling that it is possible to achieve our wants and desires...and maybe, just maybe, with the right guidance and energy source we can obtain what we thought was an impossible dream.

Because of the support of fellow travelers, and the mentors who are put in our path at the right time, we do gain the confidence and the motivation to move out of our comfort zone. We can take that next step in accomplishing our career goals and any other aspirations we may have locked away and neglected.

Now we are able to go the distance, and become the person we dared to dream of becoming.

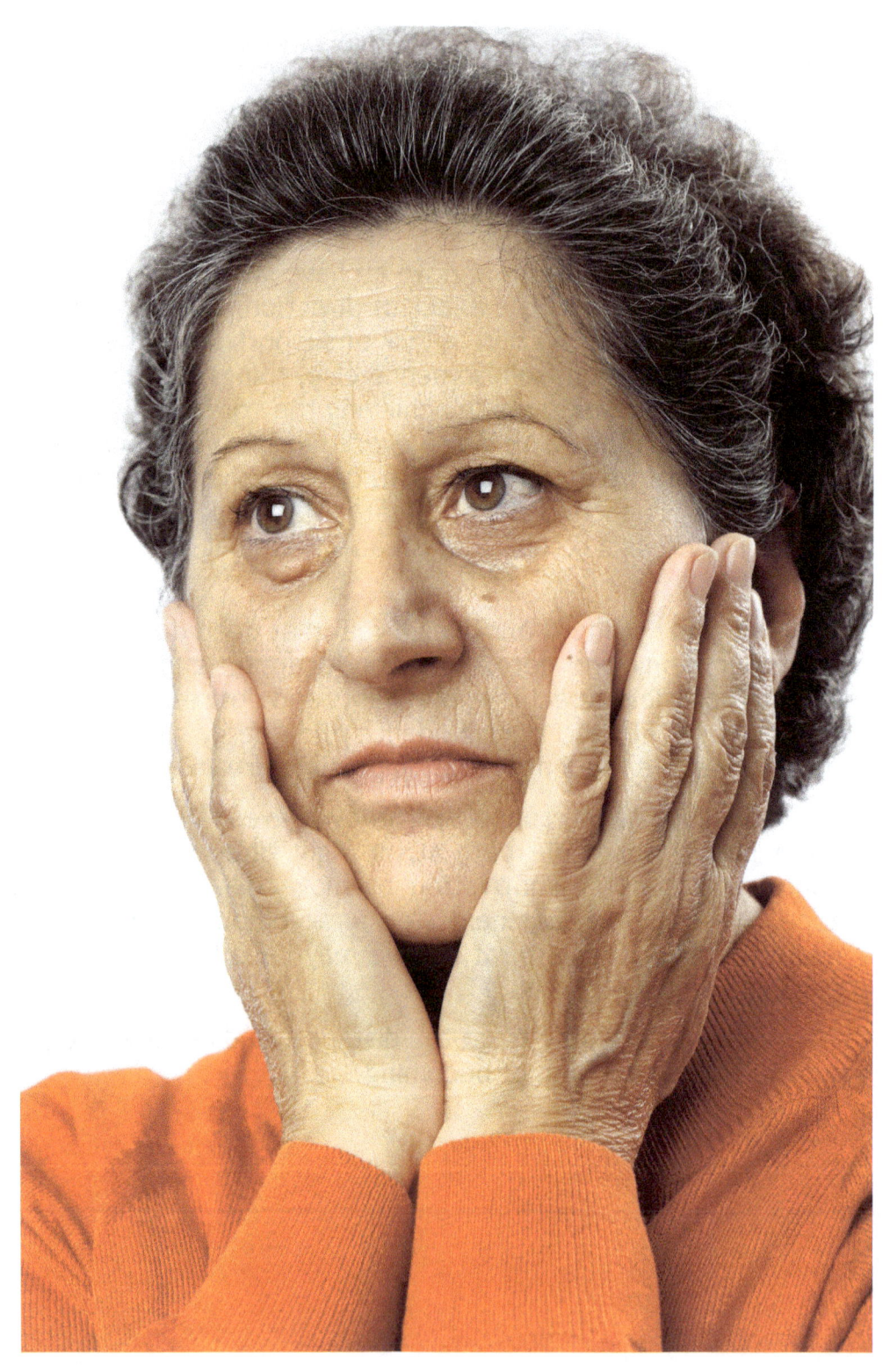

PART FOUR

SETBACKS AND CHALLENGES

DEALING WITH SETBACKS AND CHALLENGES, BEING CONFIDENT, MAKING CHANGES AND BEING OKAY

*"Escaping while you eat.
Refueling the inner you..."*

ESCAPE

Escape into the night.
Escape while they sleep,
stealing pieces of yourself back,
designated with your name;
Designed for your touch
marked selfishly for you;
Soulfully yours and for no one else.

Escaping while you eat.
Refueling the inner you…
escaping to find the strength,
and the stamina to deal with
life's everyday challenges.

Gaining back self-respect…
self-confidence…
self-esteem…
self-awareness…
self-love…
self.

RECYCLING LIFE

During the recycling period in your life, you must stop and rethink how you "think".

This is the opportunity to focus on your new given life...a chance to start all over again. A time to look at your current circumstance not as a punishment, but as a start to something exciting...and not as the end. Remember, this is your beginning...sometimes it takes some of us more tries than others...a few falls, scrapes and bruises...before we can get this right.

This time, right now, start to remember that there is a higher being holding the key to your existence. All you have to do is open up your mind, have faith, and let God exist. We learn this through meditation, prayer and being quiet. Keep in mind that as you recycle and prepare for your new journey in life, it is predestined. At no time should you have to question who to turn to in times of confusion and doubt. This fact is privy to all of us. In the beginning it was a given to each of us the moment life was breathed into our bodies. We were also given the handbook for our existence to life...the Bible. The Bible is the oldest book known to man and is used as a guide by the richest and the most scholarly of men.

When you inherited life, you also inherited the knowledge and guidance on how you should travel this road of life. In order for each of us to survive our travel through life, we must first understand that God will be with us during our times of troubles. He knows what you are confused about and where and when your "short coming" will occur. We must also earn to be still...and how to be quiet ...and how to listen in the mist of all of the confusion around us. We must learn to use the power of God which exists within, even through the pain that we may be feeling in our heart at a particular moment in time. This will enable us to receive His continuous guidance, making our travel through life as rewarding and as peaceful as it is promised.

"Hasten the quick decisions I make on impulse."

QUIET MY MIND SO THAT I MAY HEAR

Quiet my mind God,
so that I may hear Your voice.
Quiet my mind so that my thoughts and desires
connect with what you desire for me.

Quiet my mind God,
so that I may hear and receive Your instructions and guidance.

Quiet my mind,
so that I may feel the peace *that You are*.
Shut out the confusion that surrounds my thoughts,
steady my mind and spirit.

Hasten the quick decisions I make on impulse.

Guide my feet in the right direction,
so that I may step down the path which has been clearly defined,
and laid out for me .

IT'S GONNA BE OKAY

I wish that I could grab you,
hold you, squeeze you and say...
"It's Gonna Be Okay,"
"It's Gonna Be Okay."

The tears that you shed,
the pain that you feel...
Oh, how so very real.

Even if I can't grab you,
hold you, squeeze you and say...
"It's Gonna Be Okay,"
"It's Gonna Be Okay."

It still is...
"Gonna Be Okay."

PART FIVE
NEGATIVITY

CLOSING THE DOOR TO NEGATIVITY

CLOSING THE DOOR TO NEGATIVITY

Don't allow negativity to keep you from being the person you should be, and from obtaining the heights you are predestined to reach. Negative thoughts, negative people, and negative situations are all means to quick destruction! If we fall short and give into negativity, this will be the starting point to receiving, giving, and being negative.

"Renew your mind with the word of God. Forbid thoughts of failure and defeat to inhabit your mind."

NEGATIVITY

If at some point in your life you have allowed negativity to totally consume you to the point where your self-esteem is very low, then you will need to allow yourself to slowly grow back into a positive state of mine.

Start by giving yourself permission to think positive. Be thankful for the little things in life. Even when everything around you appears to be going wrong, continue to focus on the positive.

Be thankful that you can breathe...feel...smell...taste...walk. Allow the positive in you to prevail. Any positive thought, no matter how small, is a good thought.

See your negative situation turning into a positive outcome. Being positive generates positivity...causing a chain reaction of positive energy, creating a healthy attitude resulting in high self-esteem.

Remember, God is the positive force in our lives...so plug yourself into this power source and feel yourself growing stronger and stronger; see yourself overcoming.

PART SIX

THE PROCESS TO RECOVERY

"FOR I KNOW THE PLANS I HAVE FOR YOU SAYS THE LORD...PLANS TO PROSPER YOU, NOT TO HARM YOU...PLANS TO GIVE YOU HOPE AND A FUTURE."
JEREMIAH 29:11

ACHIEVING BALANCE

Meditation is a great way to achieve balance within oneself. This allows the inside to be quieted...thus, making room for harmony and calmness to co-exist. These two entities are needed in the healing process. When the body is at rest and quiet, the mind is then at peace...causing one to be focused and receptive to receive positivity from positive sources.

I find that, for me, to obtain the maximum benefits of meditation I do some or all of the following things:

- Praying in the quiet of the early morning in a serene place
- Listening to calming music
    - Spiritual music
    - Favorite slow jazz sound
    - Outdoor nature sounds especially water sounds
- Relaxing in a warm bath with soothing candles
- Walks in the park near a stream or pond
- Walking on a beach.

ACHIEVING WELL BEING

Exercise, a proper diet, vitamins and rest will benefit you greatly. You feel and look better when your daily routine is enhanced with these four essential items. By doing so, your body will be able to physically handle the everyday stresses that occur on a day-to-day basis.

"Allow your spirit to fly and soar above the obstacles that bind you."

LOVING YOURSELF FIRST

Treat yourself with a day or a hours of self-love. I find satisfaction when I can treat myself to something once or twice a month. Rewarding yourself is a means of self-gratification and I think we all should always remember that it is good and healthy to give oneself permission to take time off for self; so that you don't lose touch with feelings about one self. It's okay to relax without it being a Sunday rest day or working so hard that we are forced to take a sick day because we over did it. Go ahead...you deserve to love yourself.

- Treat yourself to a movie by yourself or with a favorite friend or loved one;

- If you have kids and it's impossible to get away, then try getting a teenager to come to the house or if you have friends who have kids trade days or hours watching each other's kids while you relax and read.

- Pamper your body by giving yourself a manicure and/or pedicure or doing something you've put-off doing because of your busy schedule taking care of the kids and the rest of the household.

ONE DAY AT A TIME

I'll take each day one day at a time, and as I come to the many bends in the road, that aren't so straight, I will shape my body to take on the formation of each curve. I will brake gently as demanded, then straighten out to continue my daily journey.

The obstacles that I will encounter will be as hurdles. Each will present a different challenge; some easier than others. But, like a sprinter, I will adjust my stride and pace myself in an effort to develop a rhythm to clear each hurdle, one by one.

My rhythm may be broken at some point; life has a way of doing that. But I'll continue to stride with God's speed, clearing those that I can clear, and trying never to look back at the fallen ones. I will refocus each time to clear the next approaching hurdle, because this hurdle, at this moment in time, is all that matters...at this time!

"God is our refuge and strength...an ever present help in trouble"
Psalm 46:1

GROUND YOURSELF IN GOD'S WORD

Ground yourself in God's word
For His word is your foundation
It is how He allows us to
Rebuild and reinvent ourselves.

It's not how many times we reinvent self...
It's the fact that we can pick ourselves
up and start all over again...this is what
makes our relationship with God so special
and through this, all things are possible.

Bathe in his word...live in His word...
"the strength and foundation of our lives."

BUILD A RELATIONSHIP WITH GOD

Build a relationship with God through prayer;
Through reading and learning his words and his promises
he set for us;

Through total submission to him; trusting in
him to guide us and to show us the way through his
word and through fellow travelers that are placed in
our path to encourage us along the way.

PART SEVEN
CHOOSING TO LIVE

AS WE TRAVEL ON OUR JOURNEY IN LIFE, WE WILL MEET FELLOW TRAVELERS NEEDING US TO REACH OUT TO THEM OR WHO WILL REACH OUT TO US IN RETURN.

WE ALL POSSESS STRENGTHS BEYOND WHAT WE EVER THOUGHT WAS POSSIBLE. WE ONLY NEED TO TAP INTO THE RIGHT POWER SOURCE.

THIS ROAD I TRAVEL

This road I travel in life maybe rough.
But, I have decided this is only to make us tough.

The decisions that I shall make will be many,
because choices are given to all of us.

I run the risk of falling...
turning around and making a mistake...But,
remembering...I am given another chance...
to get up and start all over again;
this time armed with the knowledge I did not possess before.

While traveling this road of life I will choose to smile,
because someone may smile back.

I will choose to laugh,
because I have experienced the healing affects
passed on as an antidote to my pain.

I will choose to be happy,
because sadness drains the positive energy we all possess.

I will choose to forgive,
because this will make me sensitive to the needs of others,

thus, passing on the many blessings;
that Jesus, the son of God, so unselfishly passed on to me.

I will try to be the best person God intended me to be...
loving...understanding...giving...and forgiving.

Allowing the blessings in my life to transpire;
making this road I travel more fulfilling and enjoyable.

I choose to live in the
"secret place of most high."
Psalm 91:1

I CHOOSE TO LIVE

I choose to live in the "secret place of most high" (Psalm 91:1)

The source of my strength, a refuge where I can dwell without fear or worry. A place to retreat to; to safely lay without fear, or strife. A place of peace and serenity.

I choose to live through adversity and knowing that the Lord our god is the keeper of my destiny.

I choose to live so that others can live, just as others chose to live for me. Passing on the legacy passed on to me from generation to generation, I now must dutifully accept and deliver to my children, who are still young travelers, and to the travelers I encounter along the way to the legacy of life. I, the seasoned traveler, have learned secrets of traveling life's journey with confidence and see things with more clarity when making life decisions. As a result...my life journey is a little easier and less stressful to travel.

I choose to live for those who struggle in their travels and choose not to live anymore. I choose to be their cheerleader to help them get through some of the tears and pain that they may be facing at that moment. It is now up to me to assist those I am blessed to encounter...even if it is a short encounter in time.

So, take my hand whoever is feeling weak and struggle with fear and doubt. I will try to guide you to that secret place on high, where you can hide and be safe from harm...a sanctuary to escape...a place to soothe and calm your mind. A place to grow and soon acquire and master the secret...the simple skills for traveling the road of life, where life steps may start out to be small baby steps and eventually steps of confidence and purpose.

MARY ELIZABETH GORE

OFFICE OF THE VICE PRESIDENT
OLD EXECUTIVE OFFICE BUILDING
WASHINGTON, D.C. 20501

October 9, 1996

Tiny Stallings-Clark

Dear Tiny:

Thank you so much for thinking of me during my recent trip to Allentown. I appreciate your card of poetry and wish you the best of luck in all of your endeavors.

Again, thanks for thinking of me.

Warmest Regards,

Tipper Gore

Tipper Gore

The National Library of Poetry

11419-10 Cronridge Drive • Post Office Box 704 • Owings Mills, Maryland 21117 • (410) 356-2000

Dear Tiny,

Thank you for your entry in our recent contest. Your poem was recognized by the judges as being among the best 3% of all entries judged. We are therefore pleased to award you our Editor's Choice Award for your contest entry as published in Edge of Twilight. Congratulations on your significant achievement.

Sincerely,

The National Library of Poetry

Editor's Choice Award

Presented to

Tiny Stallings-Clark

for Outstanding Achievement in Poetry
Presented By
The National Library of Poetry
1994

Cynthia Stevens, Editor   Caroline Sullivan, Editor

ABOUT THE AUTHOR

Tiny Stallings-Clark is a mother and celebrated poet. She is a graduate of Tennessee State University and works professionally as a Civil Engineer.

She is a spirit oriented motivational speaker. Tiny has spoken at many venues, including Women For Incarcerated Women, The Women Unlimited Association, Churches and various Writer's Conferences. She has also performed the Spoken Word in many setting in New York, Philadelphia and the Washington, D.C. area.

Tiny has been inducted in the International Society of Poets as a Life member and presently resides in Allentown, Pennsylvania with her family.

www.ingramcontent.com/pod-product-compliance
Lightning Source LLC
La Vergne TN
LVHW061216060426
835507LV00016B/1972